# Your Complete Forecast 2018 Horoscope

# ARIES

# Your Complete Forecast

# 2018

# Horoscope

# ARIES

BEJAN DARUWALLA

With

NASTUR DARUWALLA

Ranvir Books

HARPER element

First published in India in 2017 by Harper Element
An imprint of HarperCollins *Publishers*



P-ISBN: 978-93-5277-330-5
E-ISBN: 978-93-5277-331-2

2 4 6 8 10 9 7 5 3 1



**HarperCollins *Publishers***
A-75, Sector 57, Noida, Uttar Pradesh 201301, India
1 London Bridge Street, London, SE1 9GF, United Kingdom
2 Bloor Street East, Toronto, Ontario M4W 1A8, Canada
Lvl 13, 201 Elizabeth Street (PO Box A565, NSW, 1235), Sydney
NSW 2000, Australia
195 Broadway, New York, NY 10007, USA

Typeset in 11.5/15 Sabon
By Saanvi Graphics, Noida

Printed and bound at
MicroPrints (India), New Delhi

# Contents

# ARIES

21 March–20 April

You are a natural leader thanks to your immense energy, vitality and force. In other words, you are vibrant like Virat Kohli, sing superbly like the late K.L. Saigal and you have the comic genius of Charlie Chaplin, perhaps the greatest actor ever. This is the time to gun down all opposition and yet be humble and decent to all in your moment of victory and triumph. Yes, money and loans will come to you for property, industry, housing, arts, research, hobbies, new avenues of work, romance, sex and dealings with corporates, industries and financial houses. All this will come naturally to you. Congrats!

- **Good qualities:** Abundant physical energy, courage, honesty, independence, self-reliance, resourcefulness

- **Metals:** Iron and steel
- **Perfume:** Honeysuckle
- **Advice:** Caution and patience
- **Gem:** Amethyst, coral, diamond (coral is best)
- **Colours:** Carmine, red, scarlet, pink
- **Characteristics:** Bold and brash
- **Key word:** Pioneer, leader, executive, courageous, 'me-first'
- **Main planet:** Mars
- **Element:** Fire
- **Health:** The head and face, tension, headaches, dizziness, skin eruptions, migraines, allergies, sleep problems
- **Other qualities:** active, excitable, impulsive, optimistic, open to change and new experiences

- **Great point:** impulsive, selfish but also very generous (strange mix)
- **Flowers:** Geranium, honeysuckle
- **Countries:** England, Germany, Poland
- **Trees:** All thorn-bearing trees
- **Cities:** Florence, Naples, Verona, Marseilles

## SPECIAL MESSAGE FROM BEJAN AND NASTUR

You are independent by nature and temperament. Top position and power can be achieved. But if you are very aggressive, blunt and brash, remember that there is a danger of a big fall from power and position. The reason is Saturn, the planet of power, duty and responsibility, is in your tenth angle of name and fame.

The challenge with this sign is lack of persistence. They can be argumentative, lack tact, and have a bad temper. Since Aries rules the head and face, these areas are considered the weakest part of the body for people under this sign. Common ailments are tension, headaches, dizziness and skin eruptions. In fact, many Aries suffer from migraines and allergies too. Also, because they are indulgent, Aries need to be careful of easily gaining weight. It's a good thing he is so active! I must admit there are always exceptions to this rule.

Finances and loans will be available. Use them wisely. You will have much to do with investments, loans, funds, trusts, taxes, buildings and construction, inheritance and legacy, charitable causes, religious rites and ceremonies and pujas, tantra and mantra, prayers for the living and the dead. Take care of your health from May to July and also March. On the positive side, during the months of February, April, June, August, October and December you will be at your brilliant best. Health of parents, boss, elders will be cause for worry and concern. Take care of their health please. Overall position, power, success, loans, funds, investments, good money.

In 2018 you will have pelf and power for the simple reason that Saturn, planet of responsibility and duty, will be in your tenth angle as per Western astrology. Just for your information, Saturn will be in your tenth angle till 19 December 2020. Your symbol is the ram. The ram always climbs upwards till it reaches the top of the mountain. In the same way, you will also continue to climb till 19 December 2020. Therefore, your hard work and intensity will be well rewarded. But please try to be humble, kind, forgiving, and do not make a mountain of a molehill. That means do not take small matters to heart and do not fight over it. Save your energy for the big occasions in your life. Ganesha says this is the best advice you will ever get.

Mars is your main planet. Mars will help you tremendously from 29 January to 10 March 2017, 21 July to 5 September 2017, 17 January 2018 to 17 March 2018, 27 May 2018 to 27 June 2018, 12 September 2018 to 16 November 2018. Mars will help you in terms of energy, action, achievements and loans, funds, investments. These are your months of power, name and fame. Ganesha says please use it wisely and well and remember that in life moderation is the key to great success and even greater joy and happiness.

Ganesha says you will achieve much in your work area. Yes, loans, funds, finances and pension will be available to you. Also, your earning capacity will increase. But there is also a possibility of sudden changes in your personal and work area. This is not a contradiction. The reason is life is not simple and clear and everything does not fall into the place you want to. Life is often mysterious, has many changes and circumstances and therefore we human beings must learn to adjust to it. That is the real secret of lasting happiness. Luckily you Arians are born leaders, very brave and courageous, and therefore you will be able to fight life and come out a winner. My final word is you will be victorious if you are not very aggressive and violent. You can assert yourself but sometimes you must learn to listen to others. By doing so, you will be happy and make others happy. That is what life is all about.

## JUPITER

Jupiter in your eighth angle will have the following spin-offs: Loans, funds, joint finance, insurance, legacy and legal matters, money from different sources such as rents, rentals, lottery and hidden treasure. That does sound interesting!

Tantra and mantra, high passion and sizzling sex, taxes, real estate issues, keeping your mouth shut (otherwise there's trouble), and religious rites are indicated. Jupiter helps you get money. That's important. This same time span will also be mighty important for: a) buying/selling/renovation/decoration of house, home/shop/godown/warehouse/office and so on. Let me know, dear readers, how right I am on these counts—matters to do with inheritances, wills, codicils, estate and taxes, hundis, taking care of both health and money, cooperating with other workers, finding new sources of money and profit, maintaining secrets and confidentiality, learning to use your energies carefully and not wasting or draining it away. Finally, it is most important that you should use your talents and imagination completely.

With Jupiter in your eighth angle the other main features will be:

a) The focus – sharp and clear – is on joint finance, loans, public trusts and charity institution;

b) Your health and that of your near and dear ones could pose some problems for you;

c) A home away from home is likely;
d) Problems of legacy, dowry, hidden treasures, wills, codicils, legal documents pertaining to marriage, alimony, company laws, contracts regarding corporations, bonds, funds may crop up;
e) Tax matters related to land, building, shop, office, godown, warehouse and so on are to be taken care of;
f) The danger of low vitality, poor health, accidents, operations, wounds, injuries – once again, I must stress health concerns;
g) Lawsuits and court proceedings will have to be dealt with;
h) Also, perhaps blackmail and deceit. Jupiter will be in your eighth angle from 10 October 2017 to 8 November 2018.

## SATURN

By Western astrology Saturn will be in your tenth angle from 21 December 2017 to 22 March 2020. Therefore, it will apply to all Arians in both 2018 and 2019. Here are the details:

Saturn in your work slot prods you into probing at your career and business possibilities and outstanding success can be anticipated. Ganesha says, it is time to go all out for the kill. It could well be the time for awards and rewards for your services rendered, and for the efforts put in by you. Yes, your prestige will also soar. Your parents and kinsmen will be proud of you. Sounds good.

Saturn will be at the zenith or mid-heaven in your solar-scope. The results will be:

a) You will have to walk the talk. In other words, your words must match your actions. You can be aggressive but never abusive. You must lead without crushing the opinions of others.

b) You will meet influential people who will be able to help you.

c) The health of parents, elders, in-laws will make you anxious and worried.

d) There will be a great struggle for power, position and prestige. If you push too hard, you might take a big tumble.

e) If you neglect your home and family, you will finally suffer the consequences.

f) The law of karma will certainly operate for you. Remember, the Gita says, 'He who knows for certain that happiness and misery, birth and death are due to the effect of past actions, does not find anything to accomplish, and thus becomes free from care and is not attached, even though engaged in action.'

This is how Saturn will work for you in 2018:

a) Prestige, power, position, perks, pelf – the five Ps – you will achieve them all.

b) Responsibility in irreversible, monumental proportions will be almost thrust upon you, but that will give you authority and the ability to handle pressure; and that's ultimately important.

c) Prestige takes an immense leap; parents will figure in your scheme of things; inheritance and possessions will play a large role in your personal life; and you will learn to play spectacularly with all the latest gadgets and media of communication.

d) The health of parents and older people, in-laws, could be a cause of anxiety. This will go for your boss and superior too.

e) Both your proficiency and your performance will be at an all-time high and this should give you the necessary self-belief, confidence to achieve targets and goals. Helping you do this is what astrology is all about.

f) Honours, awards, rewards sum it up nicely.

g) Wish-fulfilment and hope – without this nothing is possible.

h) Food for the body, good health, good money; food for the mind, intellectual stimuli, food for the soul, spirituality and the sayings of the gurus – all these are important for you.

i) Old acquaintances, new friends, sweethearts and loved ones, mate and companions, all form a full circle of contentment and joy for you – for the most part.

j) Your income could come from more than one source. For this, one of the secrets would be mixing with people, socializing and fraternizing, in short, networking as they now say. Otherwise also, Saturn in this position is ideally placed for achieving this, quite paradoxically.

k) Recognition and acknowledgements of worth will come to you, and that will obviously be sweet and satisfying.

l) You must learn not to offend those who love and support you.

Not ego, but love, will put you where you aspire to be.

m) Possessions, combining substance with style, in clothes, work, home, renovation/decoration of either new or ancestral property is foretold.

n) Good news about children, and romance and hobbies and sports have a great significance for you.

o) Pious deeds, charitable acts, the elder brother, paternal uncle, the longevity of your mother, finding lost/stolen goods/valuables, treasures, lotteries and windfalls, recovery from illness and therefore, returning from hospital or medical centres, are the other vital features. Quite a handful!

## URANUS

Till 16 May 2018, Uranus will be in Aries. In other words, Uranus will be in your sign. Uranus is the planet of both revolution and evolution. Therefore, there will be big changes in your personal life very specially and this will have an effect on your profession, business and job. I personally believe that though you may feel unsettled and restless you will finally accept all the changes which circumstances bring about for you. In the long run these changes will certainly help you. From 18 May 2018, Uranus will be in your second house of finance and family. Uranus will be responsible for sudden gains and losses. It will have the greatest impact on your finances and funds. There could be a change in the nature of your job, profession or business. If it is so, do not worry. At the same time, I wish to make it clear that astrologers are not gods and what I have said about the outer planets Pluto, Neptune and Uranus may not have the full impact of what I have predicted. The other reason is that these outer planets influence countries more than individuals. Therefore, please do not worry overmuch.

## NEPTUNE

Neptune will be in your twelfth angle till 28 January 2026. Therefore, Neptune's influence will be felt in 2018. Neptune will give you inspiration, imagination. But Neptune will also result in expenses, ill health, false accusations and possibly lawsuits and illicit relationships. In short, Neptune will bring out the best and the worst in you. Beware of being cheated or of cheating others in every possible way, namely, money, women, relationships, drugs, drinks, conning and even smuggling. But Neptune can lead you to genuine spirituality, love of

God and nature and also service to the people of the world. In short Neptune is a double-edged sword specially for you Arians in 2018.

## PLUTO

Till March 2023, Pluto, the power planet, will be in your tenth angle. It is very clear that this will apply to you in both 2018 and 2019. Pluto will help you achieve name and fame, recognition and rewards. In short, Pluto, like our own Virat Kohli, will bat for you in the game of life itself. I am sure you understand the value and worth of it.

## MONTHLY ROUND-UP

**January**: Up and about, hard work, you will be ready to be on the go, be it home/office.

**February**: Fun and games, friendship and fraternity, gains and gaiety.

**March**: Too many things happening all together; see that you conserve your energy/vitality.

**April**: Month of progress, prosperity, pelf and getting things done.

**May**: Loans and funds and deals and transactions, buying/selling.

**June**: Assignments, communication, transport, ties, trips, relatives.

**July**: Home, house, family, shopping, renovation, decoration, alteration.

**August:** Trips, ceremonies, rites, name and fame, future plans.

**September:** Work, health, rewards, service, pets, projects, colleagues, promotion.

**October:** Love, marriage, lawsuits, relationships, travel, contracts, communication, enemies.

**November:** Joint finance, loans, funds, immigration, moving, shifting, capital formation, passion, sex.

**December:** Joy, publicity, travel, ceremony, functions, parties, invitations, import and export, collaboration, contacts and happiness because of abundance.

**HAPPINESS QUOTA:** 80 per cent

# WEEKLY REVIEW (BY PHASES OF THE MOON)

## 2 JANUARY: FULL MOON IN CANCER

Home, health, family matters, even concerns regarding family health or finances, or both, could be more than demanding. You may feel that the pace in the millennium is truly hectic. Go for it, Arians, but don't trample over the dreams of others. Take it slow and easy and, for Ganesha's sake, take some time off.

## 8 JANUARY: LAST QUARTER IN LIBRA

Entertainment, amusement, hobbies and creative pursuits are all favoured, along with speculation and investing in the right places. It's a time for care and caution in money matters, or with regard to valuables, documents, wills, certificates. Don't be too open about revealing your hand, even to friends. That's not the way to play the poker game of life.

## 17 JANUARY: NEW MOON IN CAPRICORN

It's time to work hard and play your cards well, make the right moves. The three Ps – power, position and your personal angle – are all in focus, after the Sun–Saturn trine of 1 January. It's a marvellous placing, and this is what it brings you. Of course, you will have to stretch yourself in many directions. Just don't spread yourself too thin.

## 24 JANUARY: FIRST QUARTER IN TAURUS

On the one hand, possessions, property, acquisitions and on the other, a higher consciousness or plane of existence. Spiritual journeys, or even actual travel to distant places, trade, export–import and of course, in today's world, communicating at all levels. Achievements made now will give a different kind of satisfaction.

## 31 JANUARY: FULL MOON IN LEO

The moon's quarter in the last period of your sun sign ushered in hectic activity. Thus, now it extends to include finance; funds, buying, selling, investments, financial planning for the millennium are the name of the game. Don't go overboard, weigh your options before making long-term commitments/plans regarding money.

## 7 FEBRUARY: LAST QUARTER IN SCORPIO

Finance, finance and finance thrice. That's the scene this week, be it household expenses, outlay in business or both – anything that touches the pocket or the purse strings. In the process, you may well pick up some possessions, fun articles, even some gadgets. You learn to juggle finances well indeed!

## 15 FEBRUARY: NEW MOON IN AQUARIUS

Chancing your arm, backing the throw of the dice in matters, financial (speculation) bull runs on the stock market, if you're a major player, and also chancing your heart. You're in the right mood for both. Optimism and confidence at an all-time high.

## 23 FEBRUARY: FIRST QUARTER IN GEMINI

An inner search, looking for the Godhead within us all or the Buddha-like nirvana is balanced, strangely enough, with getting on in social mobility (upward, of course, I said 'yuppy', didn't I?). You'll have to devote extra time and attention to money matters, definitely.

## 2 MARCH: FULL MOON IN VIRGO

A wish-fulfilment, much fun and games, even hectic socializing and yet, strange as it may seem, at the same time a search for inner values, the real you that you don't always show to the world. Love and hatred – two sides of the same coin – may both be experienced, in relationships, even in social interaction or family matters. Learning to cope is one way of strengthening your personality, Ganesha says.

## 9 MARCH: LAST QUARTER IN SAGITTARIUS

Now it's not social/familial/kinship relationships that are important but those with superiors and bosses, officials and authorities and subordinates, employees. You still need to watch the interests of the first named, though. Funds will flow in, loans and resources will be organized very smoothly, and so also will the contacts and communications trend.

## 17 MARCH: NEW MOON IN PISCES

Awards, rewards, recognition, appreciation and the benefits that come with them. Health problems of older relatives, parents, perhaps even your boss, may cause anxious moments. So also having to take disciplinary action, or inflict punishments. Perhaps at work, or in a social context. Position and power bring their own responsibility after all.

## 24 MARCH: FIRST QUARTER IN CANCER

A time when you may be attempted to be uncooperative, even harsh in your dealings with people. Financial gains come your way, but don't look for the quick buck. It's got to be the just rewards of your own efforts. Correspondence, short trips and ties will be highlighted in this period. Even shopping trips, where you're tempted to blow up some cash on trifles, fun purchases, fripperies.

## 31 MARCH: FULL MOON IN LIBRA

The monthly trend, with the moon in your sign – you will make great individual advances, but will have a tendency to pander to your own ego and pride. That won't augur well for personal and professional relationships, both of which are highlighted in this period. Some important decisions will be made, based on intellectual and career needs as well as purely personal considerations.

## 8 APRIL: LAST QUARTER IN CAPRICORN

Partnerships, law, legal cases, buying/selling (may be of property or assets), getting a commission are highlighted. Also, buildings, construction or even doing up the house. Your own interests and concerns will be paramount, but not in a selfish way. It's just that you'll watch out for yourself, your family, your home, and you will be more than active in these spheres.

## 16 APRIL: NEW MOON IN ARIES

Both business and pleasure will be motivating factors in this period. Business partnerships as well as personal ones will therefore be equally important. Love, romance, friends, passionate interludes will all yield the 'pleasure principle'. You might even have a field day at sports, if that's where your pleasure lies.

## 22 APRIL: FIRST QUARTER IN LEO

Worries about the health of older relatives, parents, even superiors will make you work harder than usual. Stress should be avoided, therefore. It's a time when your true worth, efforts, sterling qualities will all be recognized, appreciated, even rewarded. Happy times with family and kin can happen too, but it's not a time for forcing issues or having confrontations.

## 30 APRIL: FULL MOON IN SCORPIO

As I've frequently pointed out, the trend for the lunar month is usually ushered in by the new period. It will be finances – so far on the back burner – that occupy your time, energy, talents and, more so, contracts, memoranda of understanding, agreements, joint finance. Also important will be a makeover in terms of clothes, jewellery, fashion accessories, make-up, a new look – and you'll go out and 'shop till you drop'.

## 8 MAY: LAST QUARTER IN AQUARIUS

Amusements, entertaining and being feted, wined and dined, playtime with children, friends, loved ones all come together to give you a wonderful time recreation-wise. Also, a good time for making some 'fast money'. Thrilling romance too. I would say, excitement in different ways sums it up.

## 15 MAY: NEW MOON IN TAURUS

Once again, money and honey, romance and finance! Love will almost definitely be of the earthly, sensual, passionate variety, not 'the meeting of two minds' immortalized by Shakespeare. You may have a gift, legacy, windfall; unexpected gambles can pay off. It's a lucky time for securing loans, credit, leasing and even for paying off old debts.

## 22 MAY: FIRST QUARTER IN VIRGO

The theme of love continues, and once again it's time for pleasure in each other's company – joy, a celebration of life itself. You are active not just emotionally/passionately but also at work, making the right moves, the right decisions. Money matters will be more or less smooth, so all in all, a good period by the grace of Ganesha!

## 29 MAY: FULL MOON IN SAGITTARIUS

Connections, contacts (whether long-distance or direct), even calls, letters, faxes, email. Communication and information are the name of the game now. Those in the electronic and print media, in information technology, the creative arts will find this period full of promise and gains. People and places are now part of your own backyard, and so also ties with your environment.

## 6 JUNE: LAST QUARTER IN PISCES

Higher studies, research, higher learning, idealism, dabbling in the occult and spiritual. You'll be existing on a much more elevated level of consciousness, and very actively so. There may be journeys, either spiritual or actual, from which you will gain either a pilgrimage or a study tour, business travel, foreign conferences, seminars and such.

## 13 JUNE: NEW MOON IN GEMINI

You will be very focussed on the goals you have been thinking about achieving. Whether you achieve them or not is another matter, but you will know where you're going. I must point out that if these goals are not realistic, you may experience a sense of defeat, sorrow or even depression.

## 20 JUNE: FIRST QUARTER IN VIRGO

A resurgence of hope and determination, a sense of purpose, comes to you in this period of your own sign. You experience both aggression and love, pleasure, and go out to seek them in all that you do. Money matters, domestic issues find you resolute yet charming.

## 28 JUNE: FULL MOON IN CAPRICORN

It's home, family, the comforts of your hearth, your castle that you enjoy. Parents and children are in harmony with you. There may be family gatherings or outings or even perhaps a short journey to visit dear ones. Money matters will be smooth, but not spectacular. So also your health. A good time to let others do the thinking and talking, even the decision making.

## 6 JULY: LAST QUARTER IN ARIES

You want to start afresh, particularly in terms of career goals and attitudes to both profession and home. A stronger faith in yourself, more objectivity, all help, you give your best shot to your work, impervious to rivals and competitors, like Arjuna was instructed to do by Krishna in the Bhagavadgita. And you do experience much satisfaction in doing so. Ganesha sees to it.

## 13 JULY: NEW MOON IN CANCER

You look at yourself in the mirror of life very closely indeed and the important thing is, you want to like what you see. Self-improvement, physical fitness, beautification, even new make-up/hairstyle/clothes, will be spent on, both in money and in effort. You may even join a gym, sport, some health club on your way to what you consider a better you. There may also be bond, partnership, marriage, being part of a team.

## 19 JULY: FIRST QUARTER IN LIBRA

Libra is the opposite number for Aries – the sign you get on with. Here it means that you attain a certain balance in your life – home and office, work and pleasure, vocation and avocation. In personal relationships and in your marriage too, you appreciate the value of give and take as a means for promotion of harmony, particularly in money matters.

## 27 JULY: FULL MOON IN AQUARIUS

Creativity at white heat – the arts, the media, public relations, copywriting, even children and hobbies. It's a time when even procreation and a new birth are favoured. It could equally be a good time to start a new project, launch a new product, undertake a new venture. Romance too could well be the new venture. And I'm not joking. I just see you marching to a very different drummer.

## 4 AUGUST: LAST QUARTER IN TAURUS

It's back to the world of finance, money, willy-nilly. I wonder if people even stop to think what this phrase 'willy-nilly' implies – whether of your own will or against it. That's exactly it for you. Funds, joint finances, debts, even loans for the future will keep you more than busy whereas you will feel an urge for seclusion, renouncing the world, taking up meditation/worship/tantra/mantra/prayer. Ganesha will guide you.

## 11 AUGUST: NEW MOON IN LEO

A time when you'll get work done, call in favours, get results, see your efforts bearing fruit. You might be excused for feeling complacent, but that's not a good thing. Humility, charm, willingness to help will serve you better. Your popularity graph soars, so also do your spirits. You are fun to be with and there are lots of opportunities for fun and entertainment coming your way right now.

## 18 AUGUST: FIRST QUARTER IN SCORPIO

More of the same, a refill of the cocktail of the two Fs of fun and finance see you through this period as well. On the financial front, it's funds, taxes, rentals, leases, some mergers or tie-ups and fun. I hope I don't need to spell it out. It's a rare meeting of all that's best for you around this time and even business and professional interactions/meetings acquire a personal slant.

## 26 AUGUST: FULL MOON IN PISCES

It's others that you will be totally concerned with during this period and even at some cost to yourself. Social welfare, community projects and concerns, care of older people, pets, subordinates, dependents are all important. There may be a bit of change, reorganization and revamping done at work as well, but there are no hard feelings generated. You're god with people right now.

## 3 SEPTEMBER: LAST QUARTER IN GEMINI

Group activities, being part of a larger social order, organization, conferences, TV shows – all the things that make you part of the wide world vision that is almost part of you now. Into this, add the spice of higher study, original research, philosophical insights, and you've got a rare mixture. Ethical values too will be important.

## 9 SEPTEMBER: NEW MOON IN VIRGO

All the philosophy, ethics, higher values that you were interested in during the last period now crystallize into a mood of inner peace, soul searching, even metaphysical questions and esoteric insights into the art of living, if so inclined. Your concern and love for your fellow beings will be the guiding light, the raison d'être of your life.

## 16 SEPTEMBER: FIRST QUARTER IN SAGITTARIUS

It's time to travel and on the higher plane of intellectualism, if no other way. Trips will be as important to you as ties. And the ties will be those of love, matrimony, kinship, social commitment, the community – the entire gamut! You will want to communicate and commune with everything around you – even Nature!

## 25 SEPTEMBER: FULL MOON IN ARIES

All kinds of relationship will be important in this period and through the entire coming period. New bonds, ties, relationships can be forged ranging from an engagement or wedding to business or legal partnerships. Your own attitude of cooperation and conciliation will make this possible. It will make you efficient at work, and easier to get on with in general.

## 2 OCTOBER: LAST QUARTER IN CANCER

The spirit of teamwork and cooperation has you firing on all cylinders, ready to go for the kill. I mean this in terms of getting results in office concerns, domestic matters. Love and romance are another story, not so ardently followed. It's work that's all-important, and that too for its own sake, not for the monetary rewards.

## 9 OCTOBER: NEW MOON IN LIBRA

Your own sign, once again. You will put yourself on centre stage and all things that touch your life and your self-image will be emphasized during this period – your job, home, relationships, even appearance and clothes/outfits, accessories, hairdo. The works, in short. And they will all click, so that it's a time for wish-fulfilment.

## 16 OCTOBER: FIRST QUARTER IN CAPRICORN

Work and home are the twin engines of the spacecraft on which you zoom into orbit. You don't let up at all on the work front and add on all possible care for your home, family, your house, even your parents, ancestors, distant relatives. It's your own world that you seek to create and inhabit. And earn for too, adds Ganesha.

## 24 OCTOBER: FULL MOON IN TAURUS

Two different sources of power for you now. On the material level, it's money matters like loans, funds, trade, capital formation, market, share, investments. The other is the world of sorcerer and spirits of life after death, of souls in Purgatory, perhaps even the planchette or the Ouija board as you dabble in the occult and the tantric aspect of religion.

## 31 OCTOBER: LAST QUARTER IN LEO

After the mental stimulation and activity you have experienced, it's 'relax or burst' time. And relax you do, with a vengeance, letting your hair down. Romance, partying, dancing to the exotic beat of calypso/jazz/reggae/soul/hard rock, whatever gives you the most fun.

## 7 NOVEMBER: NEW MOON IN SCORPIO

With your batteries recharged, your stamina restored after having called 'time out', you're back at work! Arians have this great capacity to remain focused on their own interests and pursuits. And for you it's: a) money, income generation, rentals and property, acquiring assets that will pay handsomely later and b) making friends, making up, making love, whatever is necessary to heal the wounds of the past and make life sweet for your loved ones.

## 15 NOVEMBER: FIRST QUARTER IN AQUARIUS

Ganesha says progress and achievements come to you now. Your contacts, colleagues, companions are a source of strength, ideas, support. You may not suffer from a dearth of ideas, but bouncing them off wise, equally aware people always helps. Your ideas get polished, sharpened and acquire a cutting edge. In addition to these good connections, a truly beneficial and solid partnership could develop now, so that there is mutual gain and also shared respect and regard.

## 23 NOVEMBER: FULL MOON IN GEMINI

The love, care, concern that you aspire for (as do we all) are yours in full measure. In fact, your 'cup runneth over' with joy and warmth in relationships, family bonding, friendship. There may be the added thrill of joy from your children, a wedding to be held soon, or an engagement announced. Sports and adventure too.

## 30 NOVEMBER: LAST QUARTER IN VIRGO

It's you dancing down the streets with joyous abandon or laughing all the way to the bank. That is the vision that Ganesha conjures up before me. He adds a note of warning, as always. Don't throw caution to the winds in your elation and euphoria. Take care of your health and your purse.

## 7 DECEMBER: NEW MOON IN SAGITTARIUS

It's time for larger concerns now. You have a certain sense of security in your home, your family, your income-generating ability. You now turn to: a) spiritual and occult practices; b) social and charitable concerns, working for the public good; c) healing and nurturing others and in so doing nurturing your higher self, so that there is calm and certainty where there were doubts and anxieties.

## 15 DECEMBER: FIRST QUARTER IN PISCES

It's time for action, but a vastly different kind. All the C words – communications, connections abroad, contacts, computer technology – come together to form a single unit – creativity – and that too, truly with a capital C. All the media, all forms of self-expression, all the creative arts – you choose your own special forte and perform brilliantly and effectively.

## 22 DECEMBER: FULL MOON IN CANCER

It's time for you to get to work. And working with a will, can the rewards, recognition, results be far behind? The beauty of it all is that it's not the rewards that attract you but an inner satisfaction; the glow that comes from a job well done lights up your life in many ways. And that is the gift of the new millennium for you.

## 29 DECEMBER: LAST QUARTER IN LIBRA

The year 2018 is drawing to a close and new trends for 2019 will be ushered in. It's a time when you realize that though heaven always exceeds a man's grasp (by definition it should be so) but the joy of reaching for the stars is not possible without hard, even unremitting, work and toil. And the rewards are bound to be there. As you have found for yourself, from more or less happy experience over the past period, by the grace of Ganesha.

## Achievements 2018

By the grace of Lord Ganesh, my son Nastur found patrons in Shri Raj Kumar Jatia and his son, Shri Adarsh Jatia, the owners of Four Seasons, Mumbai, and Provenance Four Seasons Private Residences. May patience and hard work take my son to the top of the world where Shri Raj Kumar Jatia stands like a shining star. Nastur was graciously invited by the noble business tycoon, Byram Avari, of Avari Group of Hotels, Karachi, and his wife, Goshpi Avari, to attend their fiftieth wedding anniversary.

I bless prosperity upon Prayush Poddar, his father and his family. May his company, AMP Universal Realty Pvt. Ltd, prosper. He has been like a son to me.

May the grace of Lord Ganesha bless Police Commissioner Anupam Singh Gehlot of Rajkot. He has always stood by my family, in good times and bad. Peace and prosperity prevail in Rajkot because of his sincere efforts.

BJP National vice-president and Rajya Sabha member, Vinay Sahasrabuddhe is a very fine and noble gentleman. He was gracious enough to arrange a meeting with Maharashtra chief minister Devendra Fadnavis, who was dynamic and touched by the divine.

# Body Language

Ganesha believed astrology to be all about behaviour, relationships and how to handle them. Therefore, the guidelines given below should help you to understand yourself and others. Any information that adds to the knowledge of oneself is always welcome. Here are some examples of body language and its possible interpretations:

## POSITIVE VIBES

- Open arms and hands: open and receptive
- Leaning forward: interested in conversation

- Smiling or attempting to be humorous: friendly
- Eye contact with occasional, natural breaks in the stare: focused and curious
- Nodding while listening: attentive and alert
- Open palms: approachable and trusting
- Gesturing with hands while talking: genuinely involved in the conversation
- Upright shoulders: positivity

## NEGATIVE VIBES

- Crossed arms and/or legs: closed off, defensive, reserved or suspicious
- Standing with hands inside the pockets: unsure or suspicious
- Fidgeting, running one's tongue along one's teeth, playing with hair

or jewellery or tapping feet: nervous and/or bored

- Lack of eye contact or staring too intently and unblinkingly: untrustworthy
- Leaning back: uncomfortable
- Clasping hands behind the head while leaning back: seeking power
- Drooping shoulders: unsure

# Colours of Life

Ganesha believes that life is like a rainbow. Life is like nature, full of abundance and variety. The best part of it is you can actually experiment with the colours given below and have fun. Here, we combine abundance and a variety of colours for joy, use, experience.

- **Energetic:** Red
- **Sporty:** Red, orange
- **Exuberant:** Orange
- **Active:** Orange, yellow
- **Modern:** Yellow

- **Invigorating:** Green, yellow
- **Sunny:** Green, yellow
- **Fresh:** Green
- **Luminous:** Blue, Green
- **Hypnotic:** Blue
- **Regal:** Blue, violet
- **Exotic:** Violet
- **Playful:** Red, orange, violet, yellow
- **Vibrant:** Green, red

(Your astrologer admits that this colour system is *not* his own.)

# Important Dates

I have always believed that the fear of failure has never led to advancement of knowledge. These dates and directions may differ from the various trends and forecasts mentioned elsewhere in the book. A different direction is being pursued here. This is a totally different ball game. This is to be taken as an experiment on a mass scale with the readers themselves as guinea pigs (willingly, I hope).

Please remember, as a rule, your birth month and the seventh month from it (including itself) will be hectic. For example, if your birth month is March, the seventh from it will be September. There will be tremendous franticness in both these months.

**January**: 3–4, 8–9, 11–15, 17–18, 21–22, 25–27, 30–31

**February**: 1, 4–6, 9–10, 13–15, 18–19, 22–23, 27–28

**March**: 3–4, 7–9, 12–13, 16–17, 20–21, 25–26, 30–31

**April**: 4–5, 8–9, 12–13, 16–17, 20–21, 25–26, 30–31

**May**: 1–2, 5–6, 9–11, 14–15, 19–20, 24–25, 28–30

**June**: 2–3, 6–7, 10–11, 15–16, 20–21, 25–26, 29–30

**July**: 2–3, 6–7, 10–11, 15–16, 20–21, 25–26, 28–30

**August**: 1, 4–5, 8–10, 13–15, 19–20, 23–24, 27–29

**September:** 1, 5–6, 10–11, 15–16, 19–20, 23–24, 27–29

**October:** 2–3, 7–8, 12–13, 16–17, 21–22, 25–26, 29–31

**November:** 3–5, 8–9, 13–14, 17–18, 21–22, 26–27

**December:** 1–2, 6–7, 10–11, 14–15, 18–20 (everything meets during 18–20 December, it is the focal point), 23–24, 28–29

**Special Note:** For Aries, February is the launch pad to the entire year.

# Secret of Life

Ganesha (whom you may refer to as Allah/Christ/Zoroaster or by any other name) is the ignition key of life's car. To start and launch in the name of Ganesha is to assure success and glory. The power, the dazzling light to see visions, have prophetic dreams, and are all bestowed upon us by Ganesha.

Ganesha says the secret of life is in the ability to change with the changing times. In other words, it is the ability to adapt and adjust to situations, conditions, surroundings, climate change, relationships, and science and technology. His second secret is to keep an open mind. Others are most welcome to their own opinion. The third and final secret is to be true to yourself.

## Success Secret of No. 17

Ganesha says the secret of life and astrology is to 'Observe! Observe! Observe!' Angela Merkel of Germany, our own Narendra Modi, former US first lady Michelle Obama, and Muhammad Ali, the world's greatest boxer, were all born on the seventeenth days of their birth months. Here is a picture of the tarot card of number seventeen, called the 'Star'. We can see a lady pouring water on the Earth and providing nourishment. To me the lady is the symbol of the great feminine principle which rules the entire world. There are seven stars in the card. As we all know, seven is the mystical number of spirituality, growth and development.

Narendra Modi, 17 September

Michelle Obama, 17 January

Angela Merkel, 17 July

Muhammad Ali, 17 January

To observe is to see completely and carefully. If you observe the above, you will find that all these four individuals are born on the seventeenth. Secondly, the first alphabet of either the first name or the surname in each case is 'M'. The tarot card points towards a great and powerful destiny. Therefore, for all these reasons I believe that the number seventeen and the letter 'M' go with greatness and glory. Yes, I agree that it may not hold true for all the persons born on the seventeenth of various months. I am open-minded.

Is it but a coincidence or is it fate and destiny? I leave it to you to decide.

# World Horoscope 2018

Ganesha says cooking is an art. The challenge lies in the ever-changing nature of the ingredients, the temperature, the flavour, the aroma and the very style of cooking.

The ingredients are: artificial intelligence; healing broken bodies, mind, and spirit (most important); managerial skills of a high order; immense strides in medicine and specially brain power; space travel; robots; biopharmaceuticals; origin of life; God vs technology; climate change; and finally the marriage of technology and humanity.

Let me put it in very simple terms. The years from 2018 to 2020 will have both revolution and evolution. Change is the only constant law of nature. Not only will we survive, we will also prevail. The planets responsible for this constant change in direction are Jupiter, Saturn and Pluto. Jupiter means prosperity, Saturn means inevitable changes and Pluto means drastic and unavoidable situations and effects. These three planets are the trio of the cardinal, ambitious, ruthless sign of duty and responsibility: Capricorn. In short, Capricorn is the father who uses a big stick for others but unhappily not for himself. That is the comedy and the tragedy of the Capricorn sign.

As I have said earlier, this is not the right time for Donald Trump. His world view is one that is corrupted by imagination, illusion and, sometimes, hallucination. The Capricorn North Korean President Kim Jong-un will face terrible times and will be completely defeated in the end by fate. Vladimir Putin of Russia and Theresa May of the UK will find it very difficult to hold on to power. Angela Merkel of Germany is simply wonderful and effective. There is a distinct possibility of a settlement or an understanding between the Jews and the Muslims in 2018 itself. God bless them both. Changes in the regimes in Pakistan and the UK appear certain. In the words of Paul Brenton, 'There is peace behind the tumult, goodness behind the evil, happiness behind the agony.' Nobody has a monopoly over truth, love, justice, mercy, kindness and happiness.

India is certainly tolerant up to a certain extent, but it would be wise, practical and necessary to be much more tolerant and far less rigid and orthodox. Water recycling and the treatment of sewage will be a big changer for our country in 2018 and 2019. It will lead to happiness. I say this in all humility and love for Bharat Mata as I am her child. I certainly bow my head at the feet of Bharat Mata. India comes under the planet of Saturn causing changes that are radical, effective, certain. Our Narendra Modi will hold his own against the world. But India will undergo numerous changes, a few of them could be painful but are necessary in the bigger scheme of events. Not religion but responsibility, duty and development will be the three salient features of India in the coming years.

To be happy we must keep an open mind. Perhaps, I say perhaps the best years will be 2018 and 2021. The year 2021 is most certainly the one when science and technology reign supreme and change the very fabric and direction of all of us. Possibly this is the greatest prediction your humble Ganesha devotee will ever make.

## Salute and Tribute

A salute and tribute to the following people:

- Gujarat chief minister Vijay Rupani, in whom I saw a perfect balance in the lines of fate, head and heart on his palms. A great heart and a finely tuned mind.
- Philanthropist and naturalist Firdoz Khambhatta, a dangerously handsome, sharp and brilliant man.
- The lovely Meher Medora, firm of purpose and understanding and sympathetic of heart.

- Aravind Mothi and his sister, Anu Mothi, for offering to make a documentary on my life.
- Hotelier Raj Kumar Jatia for his hospitality and courtesy.
- Behram Mehta for his business acumen fused with immense humility and humanity.
- Jay Shah, son of BJP president Amit Shah, for coming to my house and seeking the blessings of all the mighty spirits and energies of each and every religion.
- The very cultured, civilized, and well-informed education minister of Gujarat, Shri Bhupendra Chudasma for his wisdom as well as his faith in Ganesha.
- Usha Nair, Dr Sunny Shah, Nashit Afroze and their team at the International Human Rights Council for services rendered to NGOs all

over the world. I was very humbled to receive a trophy from them, one I shall always treasure.

- Prince Lakshyaraj of Udaipur for his constant endeavour to help thousands of people through education, NGOs and by example for leading an exemplary life.
- My personal blessings by calling upon all the energies of the world to bless my adopted son Chirag and his fiancée Nikita. They are gems.
- I bow very humbly to my guru, Vashishth Mehta, for coaching me across the path of astrology and spirituality.
- Kudos to Neeraj Bajaj, the son of my late friend and patron Ramkrishna Bajaj, and Dadi Mistry for helping the needy, the weak and the helpless in every possible way. Both are truly magnanimous people.

- Raja Vikram Singh of Jambughoda for his humour and resounding laughter. No wonder his Jambughoda resort is doing immensely well.
- Just as this book is going to press, I met Shiroy and his fiancée, Avasti. Avasti specializes in fashion. Shiroy is an absolute gentleman.
- Lastly, I salute and pay my tribute to all those who seek and serve the cause of peace and goodwill to humanity. To me this is certainly the final word.

## About the Author

Born on 11 July 1931, Bejan Daruwalla lives with his wife and their three children. Now, eighty-six years old, he is regarded as one of the hundred greatest astrologers of the last century, as acknowledged by *The Millennium Book of Prophecy* (HarperCollins), having accurately predicted the electoral victory of Narendra Modi at the Kanoria Art Centre, Ahmedabad, on 29 March 2012. Bejan featured on *Hard Talk India* on BBC in August 1999. On 10 December 2010, Bejan was featured in *The Job: Corporate Astrologer* in London's *Financial Times*. Bejan was also awarded the Dr Babasaheb Ambedkar Noble Award on 19 April 2017. Giving Bejan more joy and material achievement was shaking hands with His Holiness the Dalai Lama in December 2013, a moment unforgotten and overwhelming. Bejan has one firm belief: tolerance. He believes everyone has the right to their own ideas and opinions; the perspective of others, even and especially if it differs from one's own, must always be respected.

# Important Announcement

Our Ganesha devotee Bejan Daruwalla has moved from Mumbai to Ahmedabad. His Ahmedabad address is:

Bejan Daruwalla
Astrologer and Columnist
C/o Nastur Daruwalla
A-5, Spectrum Towers
Opposite Police Stadium
Shahibag
Ahmedabad 380004
India

**Telephone**

079-32954387

09825470377

08141234275

**Email**

info@bejandaruwalla.com

bejandaruwalla@rediffmail.com

Website: www.bejandaruwalla.com